Dr Denry Machin

THE WISDOM OF HEADS

short advice for school leaders

PEDAGOGUE Publishing
Second edition, 2020
ISBN: 978-1-8381361-1-6

Cover by: Jelena Marcetic
Image Credits: Cyn Thomas
Typesetting: Shabbir Hussain

CONTENTS

FIRST THOUGHTS

For those of you about to embark on the leadership journey:

> "IT'S A DANGEROUS BUSINESS, FRODO, GOING OUT YOUR DOOR. YOU STEP ONTO THE ROAD, AND IF YOU DON'T KEEP YOUR FEET, THERE'S NO KNOWING WHERE YOU MIGHT BE SWEPT OFF TO."
>
> J.R.R. Tolkien, The Lord of the Rings: The Fellowship of the Ring

ABOUT ME

> CAUSE IT'S A BITTERSWEET SYMPHONY,
> THAT'S LIFE
> TRYING TO MAKE ENDS MEET
> YOU'RE A SLAVE TO MONEY THEN YOU DIE
> I'LL TAKE YOU DOWN THE ONLY ROAD I'VE EVER
> BEEN DOWN

(The Verve; Bitter Sweet Symphony)

It was a long drive. Perhaps an hour or so each way. It was 1997 and The Verve had just released Bitter Sweet Symphony. I had the album on hard rotation in my car.

I was driving to my first teacher training placement. The journey was one of anticipation, excitement and, on the days when I was being observed by my mentor, the usual new teacher anxieties.

I loved every minute of my training. It was a year spent honing my craft and learning my subject – a year spent gaining confidence in the classroom and confidence in myself as a teacher. Surviving the bottom-set on a Friday afternoon was a sign of progress; getting them to actually learn something was a first taste of teachings immense rewards.

In the twenty years since, I have enjoyed highs and struggled through lows. I have helped under-achievers improve and over-achievers restore. I have counselled and cajoled. I have helped exam groups through to outstanding results and been disappointed at unused potential. I have risen through the ranks, and been privileged to lead, train and support other teachers. I have camped, skied, cross-dressed, snorkeled, danced, sung, laughed, and cried. All in the service of education.

You have probably had similar experiences.

As teachers, we make a difference. We have the opportunity to significantly improve lives. The children in our care benefit from our knowledge, our experience, our compassion, our guidance and our direction.

They also benefit from our wisdom.

This book is an attempt to share some wisdom for the benefit of aspiring school leaders. My experience is pooled with that of other senior school leaders - the combined and curated 'Wisdom of Heads'.

And, for those who like such things, here's the formal biography:

Formerly Head of Upper School at Harrow Bangkok, Denry now works for the Harrow International group. Denry also supports the University of Warwick with their Asia-based teacher training programmes and serves on the Governing Body of an international school in Malaysia. Denry is a published author, including co-authorship of DK's bestselling 'The Business Book'.

Dr Denry Machin

INTRODUCTION

This book isn't a '*how to*' of school leadership. It's a '*how do*'.

How do this sample of school leaders approach Headship, and what have they learnt along the way?

What I offer is a curated collection of thoughts and advice from a diverse group of school leaders, with differing levels of different experiences. The collected musings of school leaders; snippets from their attempts to master Headship.

Not everything will be relevant to you. And you won't agree with everything. That's OK; in fact, that's a good thing.

The comments that immediately resonate may confirm what you already know, but you will get much more from the book if you reflect on the comments you don't agree with as much as those you do. The comments which strike a nerve, which cause you pause, or which require reflection are potentially powerful. You don't have to agree with them, but understanding and challenging *why* you disagree is how you develop wisdom.

There's no expiration date on the advice in this book. In the following pages, you'll find advice from 30-something high-flyers and seasoned veterans in their 60s and 70s. The hope is that each time you pick up this book something new will grab you, shake your perception of leadership, illuminate your follies, confirm your intuitions, or offer new wisdom.

The entire spectrum of schooling can be found in this book, from hilarious to heartening, from failure to success, from mundane to magical.

May the wisdom herein make you a wise Head.

HOW TO USE THIS BOOK

This isn't a book you read cover-to-cover.

It's a book you flick through. A book you return to. Whether electronic or in old-fashioned ink, it's a book you jot notes in. My hope is that you will fill it with doodles, highlights and scribbles, virtual or real.

It's that kind of book.

I want you to skip anything that doesn't grab you. Don't waste your time on sections that are not relevant to you. Jump around. It's a buffet to choose from. Borrow liberally, combine creatively, create your own bespoke compendium of wisdom.

The book has fourteen short sections. Eleven are based on the survey questions, three offer related advice for aspiring leaders. There is plenty of overlap across the sections. Where patterns emerged across the responses, I've noted them. My own thoughts, insights or musings related to the comments are in parenthesis.

Heading each section is a quote, usually a famous quote by a famous person. These quotes are not filler. Each was deliberately chosen, and deliberately placed in front of its respective section, to prompt reflection. Pondering these quotes is part of the process.

Most sections also start with a short preamble; these thoughts and words are my own. They set the stage for the wisdom which follows.

Humour

I've included small doses of humorous, odd and quirky comments; advice to purchase "a stock of high-quality shirts (pink preferred)" for example. First of all, we are teachers, it's supposed to be fun. Second, if this book was all stern looks and folded arms, you'd remember very little - information without emotion isn't retained.

URLs, Resources and Websites

Where specific resources or websites are mentioned I haven't included URLs.

We have all been there. You patiently type out an internet address, only to discover that the link is dead. You assume that you typed incorrectly. You check and retype. Still dead. It's not you, it's the link.

Frustrating.

It's also a huge waste of your time.

I have provided enough detail that a quick Google search of the book title, term or resource should take you to the relevant website.

THE QUESTIONS & LEARNING HOW TO ASK QUESTIONS

> "THE STUPIDITY OF PEOPLE COMES FROM HAVING AN ANSWER FOR EVERYTHING. THE WISDOM OF THE NOVEL COMES FROM HAVING A QUESTION FOR EVERYTHING."
>
> Milan Kundera, The Unbearable Lightness of Being

The questions are the backbone of this book. They do the heavy lifting.

Asking good questions is a skill. If you want wise words, you need to ask wisely worded questions.

To uncover the Wisdom of Heads I needed a series of great questions. Simple and quick to answer but probing. Questions which inspire interesting anecdotes and stories. Questions which result in insightful and actionable advice. Questions which combine the collected wisdom into useful counsel.

From an initial list of 30, the questions were whittled down. Through multiple trial runs with colleagues, the final choices were selected on the basis of quality - some yielded better responses than others. Each was then fine-tuned, iterated and improved; the wording of each edited and reformed. The order was also adjusted. If questions elicited better responses later in the set, they were repositioned.

With the questions refined, the survey was shared far and wide.

Over 200 school leaders responded: some to all questions, others to one or two; some at length, others with more brevity. A few of the contributors are named at the back of this book, others wished to remain anonymous. My thanks and gratitude goes to all of those who took the time to share their wisdom.

The examples provided with the questions are those shared with the school leaders. These were intended as brief prompts, offering inspiration and guidance. Each example was itself an early response to the draft survey.

The exact questions are listed below. It is important to read them in full here, as I shorten them and contain them within prose at the start of each chapter.

THE QUESTIONS

Are there any daily routines that an aspiring school leader should adopt?

[Example: "I try to be at the school gate at morning drop-off and evening collection as often as possible"]

Are there any books (educational or otherwise) you would recommend to aspiring school leaders?

[Example: "Michael Fullan's 'Leading in a Culture of Change' is essential reading for any aspiring school leader"]

Can you give any examples of quotes or phrases that have guided your approach to school leadership?

[Example: "If you put your mind to it, you can accomplish anything"]

Are there any resources you would advise aspiring senior leaders to invest in?

[This could be magazine subscriptions, time spent at conferences, or even something like a good pair of shoes!]

Do you have any 'go to' interview questions? What are they?

[Example: "I ask candidates whether they have experienced failure, and how they responded"]

Do you have any tips for maintaining (some degree of) work-life balance?

[Example: "Protect at least one night of the week from school-related work/events"]

In your experience, what are the biggest mistakes newly appointed school leaders make?

Can you relate any interesting or unique stories that exemplify the challenges and joys, highs and lows of school leadership?

Have you made any mistakes in your career that have made a difference to your practice thereafter? Can you provide an example?

What are the biggest myths, fallacies or fads you see in educational leadership?

What leadership advice would you give to your 30-year old self?

Is there any other advice or guidance, not covered in the previous questions, that you would like to offer to aspiring school leaders?

ASKING BETTER QUESTIONS

Asking better questions is a skill you can, and should, develop. No book can give you all of the answers, but, alongside the wisdom contained in these pages, this book can help you to ask better questions.

As a school leader you will need to ask lots of questions. You will ask questions when interviewing new staff. You will ask questions when talking to students, teachers and parents. You will be asked questions by your school Board, and you will need to ask questions in return.

Good questions lead to better answers. Bad questions halt, freeze, deflate, and derail thinking.

Questioning is a uniquely powerful tool. Framed properly, a good question can kickstart a process of inquiry. Questions spur learning and the exchange of ideas. They fuel innovation and performance improvement. They build rapport and trust among team members. And they mitigate risk by uncovering unforeseen risks and threats. As Eric Schmidt, CEO of Google, puts it:

> "WE RUN THIS COMPANY ON QUESTIONS, NOT ANSWERS."

The purpose and practice of questioning has its roots in ancient philosophic traditions. Socrates is well known for using questioning to probe the validity of an assumption, to analyse the logic of an argument, and to explore the unknown. Instead of lecturing them, Socrates used questions to educate students by drawing out their understanding of a subject.

So, questioning is important. But, how to develop good questioning skills?

The first step in becoming a better questioner is simply to ask more questions. Of course, volume doesn't determine quality though: type, tone, sequence, and framing also matter. Let's consider each in turn.

Question types

A 2018 Harvard Business Review article by Alison Wood Brookes and Leslie K John revealed four types of questions:

- introductory questions (example: "How are you?");

- mirror questions (example: "I'm fine. How are you?");

- full-switch questions (which change the topic entirely);

- and follow-up questions (which solicit more information).

Although each type is found in natural conversation, follow-up questions are the ones with magic powers. They signal that you are listening, care, and want to know more. People interacting with a leader who asks lots of follow-up questions tend to feel respected and heard.

Ideally, follow-up questions should be open-ended. No one likes to feel interrogated - and closed questions can force people into a yes-or-no corner they want to fight their way out of. Open-ended questions counteract this feeling; they open up the possibility for broad and expansive answers. Examples of open questions are:

- Why do you think this happened?

- What might have caused this problem?

- How can you avoid this happening in the future?

- Why do you think s/he feels that way?

- Are there other possibilities should we consider?

Follow-on questions should be followed-up with more questions. The temptation is to jump in with our opinions, responses, conclusions or suggestions. However, as we listen carefully to the answers, we should formulate further questions. We can use closed questions to get specific

Sequence

Good questions in the wrong order get bad responses. Conversely, good questions in the right order get great responses.

Consider the opening question to my series. I didn't want to scare busy people off with a heavy opener. The routines question gives scope for chunky and useful responses, but it's easy. In the early trials with colleagues this was the most frequently answered question; most leaders have some form of routine or ritual that they can quickly recall without too much thought.

We tend to sequence questions naturally for interviews: easy first, harder later. But, could we sequence them better? Are the 'hard' questions in the right order? Could they be resequenced into an order which creates a narrative, opening up the interviewee as they reveal more about themselves?

Or, when being interviewed, could you ask questions (when prompted) in a sequence which unpicks the nature of the school/position you are applying to?

We tend to take the order of questioning for granted. But, with a little extra thought we can leverage sequencing as the basis for better answers.

Framing

As with sequencing, good question framing improves response quality.

Research by Julia Minson, the University of Utah's Eric VanEpps, Georgetown's Jeremy Yip, and

Wharton's Maurice Schweitzer indicates, for example, that people are more likely to give honest responses if questions are framed pessimistically ("the department will need some new equipment soon, correct?") rather than optimistically ("you have enough equipment, right?").

Now, of course, if you want the answer to be "yes, we have enough equipment" (regardless of whether that is true or not) then you should frame the question optimistically. But, the point stands. Framing matters.

Consider again student (or staff) discipline issues. "What do you think happened?" will probably get a better response than, "Are you responsible for this disaster?" Avoid being inquisitorial and intrusive; do not ask accusatory questions. Frame your questions in a friendly and unthreatening way.

People also tend to be more forthcoming when given an 'out' (an escape) in a conversation. For example, if students are told that they won't get into trouble for their answers they tend to respond more honestly, at least to some extent.

Try to practice framing questions in everyday conversations. Instead of telling someone something, frame a question which leads to a two-way dialogue. Intelligent questions stimulate, provoke, inform and inspire. Good questions produce a whole greater than the sum of their parts. Questions help us to teach, as well as to learn.

As Einstein famously said:

"QUESTION EVERYTHING"

References

Alison W. Brooks and Leslie K. John (2018) Do Your Employees Feel Valued, Harvard Business Review, May-June 2018

Julia A. Minson, Eric M. VanEppsb, Jeremy A. Yipc and Maurice E. Schweitzerd (2018) Eliciting the truth, the whole truth, and nothing but the truth: The effect of question phrasing on deception, Organizational Behavior and Human Decision Processes, Volume 147, July 2018

ROUTINES AND RITUALS:
GET OUT OF THE OFFICE

Are there any daily routines an aspiring school leader should adopt?

Get out of the office.

Across the contributions, one theme was clear: Principals need to have presence.

A Principal with presence is visible. But, not in the panoptical sense. Being visible improves 'soft supervision' of teachers and students, and improves accountability, but that isn't its purpose. Presence isn't about catching teachers or students out; a Principal with presence isn't a threat.

A Principal with presence is emotionally engaged and actively involved. They take an energetic interest in what is going on. They walk the corridors, sit in on classes and join activities. They might even, if possible, do some teaching – or at least the occasional 'cover' lesson.

Being seen at the school gate, in the corridors, at parents' meetings, in the staff room and at sports events is critical.

A wise Principal understands that presence is more than just being present.

A few selected quotes:

"...it is important to get out of the office as much as possible and be seen."

"I try to show my face at morning drop-off and after school pick-up; a kind of reassurance tactic to our ever-demanding parents"

"Every morning I welcome students as they enter the school. It's simple and not very noteworthy, but it does set my mind straight about why I'm there. For the children, on those rare days I'm not there to greet them, it gets noticed."

"Be in classrooms daily!"

"Being present - at the lunch hall, in the staffroom, at events. That presence should be positive, supportive, collegial and kind. Most of all, authenticity is the aim. The school leader who is box ticking their way towards presence is easily caught out."

"Be available: have your office door open."

"I find a stroll through the school canteen invaluable in building relations with students."

"You must walk the campus at least once a day. In a brisk campus walk you can cover a great deal of ground and it reassures people that a) you're still alive and b) interested in teaching and learning. Take a notebook with you; it can save a lot of email traffic if people know they will see you around."

"I teach one class and have one duty per week, enabling greater empathy with staff and the demands on them."

"Be in the hallways as much as possible. People need to see your smile."

Prioritise, communicate and be consistent

As well as being visible, the Principals also shared a range of other daily rituals and productivity routines. Some are small tweaks, others are more philosophical:

"I write out my schedule for the day, and my priorities, before my first appointment. It helps me to focus on the most important tasks."

"I like to end the day by ruthlessly prioritising my to-do list, highlighting items that must get done the next day. Inevitably I get to others lower down the list on most days."

"Get in early. Be prepared for the day, whatever it brings."

"Be at school before the teachers and students."

"An early start and a chat to staff over a cup of coffee in the staff room, if the luxury of time allows."

"Always follow-up after meetings, get back to people to let them know what is happening."

"Share your calendar with staff."

"I work on 'active constructive responding' whenever I can. When with colleagues I let them do the talking, while I listen and respond positively. It sounds easy, but I find that in a busy school it takes a lot of concentration to act in this way."

"Know the names of the children [of as many children as possible] and be known to them."

"Take notes during all meetings no matter how large or small. This will help you stay engaged in the moment instead of thinking about the next task."

"Being consistent with all colleagues and pupils. Taking a stand when it matters."

"Once a day, a school leader should experience 'the school' in the same way others do: have lunch with students, visit the medical centre, pop into lessons, take a lesson (and make it a tough class!), invigilate an exam, do a cover lesson…"

"For any email or post, at the point of opening it either forward it, file it, trash it or reply to it."

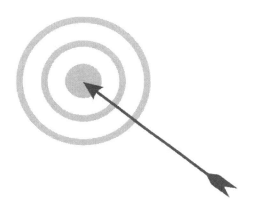

LEADERS ARE
EFFECTIVE
IF…

"WHENEVER YOU FIND YOURSELF ON THE SIDE OF THE MAJORITY,
IT IS TIME TO REFORM (OR PAUSE AND REFLECT)." | **Mark Twain**

The focus of this chapter is effectiveness. Respondents were asked to complete the sentence

'School leaders are effective if...'.

Their responses reflect signs of personal effectiveness. School effectiveness should (hopefully) follow, but I wanted to know what makes leaders themselves effective.

While not designed as such, the responses provide a loose 'checklist' against which you could compare your own leadership. Or, maybe, the comments will inspire habits that you may wish to adopt yourself.

As a school leader, you are effective if:

"You spend time with students at least weekly."

"You know at least some of the student's names."

"You visit classrooms at least weekly."

"You attend assemblies, even if you don't take them."

"You (occasionally) eat lunch with teachers (and students)."

"You know the names of janitors, chefs and gardeners etc. (in other words, you are connected to the support staff)."

"You respect how busy teachers are, but don't tell them how busy you are (for the most part, they don't care…that's why you get paid more)."

"You tell teachers to take a break. Example: I once told the teachers that the school would be closed, i.e. they wouldn't be let into the buildings, for four days of a five-day half-term. We had just been through an inspection and everybody needed, and deserved, a rest."

"You speak to parents at least weekly."

"You never cancel a meeting - it suggests you have nothing important to say."

"You have a system for managing your calendar."

"Your standard of dress sets an example to teachers and students."

"You have attended a conference in the last two years."

"You have undertaken some professional development in the last year."

"If a member of staff completes a Master's degree, and absolutely if they complete a Doctorate, you take an active interest – ideally, you would read as much of their work as time allows. If we don't value teachers who learn, then what message does that send about the value of learning in general?"

"Teachers include you in conversations, both professional and personal."

"You muck in/get your hands dirty/spend time in the trenches."

"You respect a teacher's choice to move on [to a new school]; you value and celebrate the contribution your school has made to their professional growth."

"You are visible. [see also: Routines & Rituals]"

"You don't shy away from difficult or controversial decisions."

"You conduct at least some appraisals, and not just those of senior staff."

"You are regularly appraised by a diverse body of staff (i.e. a 360 appraisal)."

"You seek input from diverse stakeholders."

"When you look at your senior management team, they are not all mirror images of you [i.e. you have recruited for diversity]."

But:

"You have a life outside of education"

"You are not distracted by (too many) outside commitments (chairing association body committees etc.)."

"You know Groupthink when you see/hear it, and you seek to avoid it."

"You sometimes green-light projects / initiatives you may not fully agree with (i.e. you know you are not always right)."

"You own up to your mistakes, and you own the consequences."

"You are professional, but you know when to drop the act. You don't try to spin everything, and you acknowledge BS, even when it's your own."

"You talk about the school, sharing its successes, with (non-school related) friends. But you also know when to shut up!"

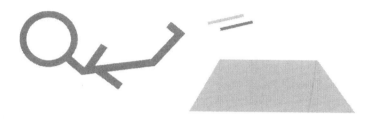

NEWBIE MISTAKES

"QUICK DECISIONS ARE UNSAFE DECISIONS." | **Sophocles**

Your first year in a leadership post is the honeymoon period. Staff will overlook your mistakes, and will hopefully cut you a little bit of slack.

That's a good thing, because newbie mistakes are common. They are also, to some extent, necessary. Mistakes are how we learn.

However, to help you avoid bringing your leadership honeymoon to a sudden, inglorious close, I wanted to know what mistakes experienced school leaders see new ones making.

By far and above, mistakes related to change management were the most popular response.

A few examples:

"Trying to change things every year - moving fast, only to then have to slow down."

"New leaders try to do everything at once. Take your time, get to know the school culture. Changes are then understood as coming from an understanding of the school rather than as an imposition."

"Trying to make changes too quickly. You need to listen, observe and ask questions (for at least one school year) first."

"Changing things before they have built relationships with people."

"Believing they need to reinvent the school in their first year; look, listen and learn first."

Other common newbie mistakes:

"Thinking they have to have the answers to all the questions."

"I think that a lot of leaders lose sight of their teaching roots far too quickly."

"Making the job about 'them'. School leaders need to be driven by vision, not ego."

"Trying too hard to be the boss. Teachers are the hardest people of all to manage."

"There are some new leaders who get pleasure out of reprimanding staff and being seen to be hard and tough, although occasionally necessary, it is seldom the only way to solve an issue."

"Believing that they should respond to emails immediately."

"Tackling everything that is wrong instead of focusing on what is going to make the most difference in their students' achievement, positive experiences and well-being. In other words, a new leader should focus on the good as well as the bad."

"Lack of delegating which can be a sign of lack of trust, or the ego of being the only one who can do the task, etc."

"A lack of communication."

"Trying too hard to be liked."

"Trying to please everyone."

"Presenting the plucking of low hanging fruit as miraculous."

"New school leaders often set themselves unrealistic and perfectionist expectations. Things take time. Be patient."

"Judging staff too quickly; try to avoid 'pigeonholing'"

"Micro management. Trying to do everything. You need to delegate and prioritise."

LESSONS LEARNED

"NO MATTER HOW MANY MISTAKES YOU MAKE, YOU ARE STILL WAY AHEAD OF EVERYONE WHO ISN'T TRYING." | Tony Robbins

Following on from newbie mistakes, I wanted to know what mistakes the leaders themselves have made.

Remember, these are all successful serving or retired school leaders. But they are not perfect. Wisdom doesn't come from having no weaknesses; it comes from knowing your weaknesses and addressing them. Those weaknesses are often revealed in our mistakes.

The ability to reflect on our mistakes, to learn from them, to move on from them, and to grow because of them are traits of an accomplished leader - traits of a wise Head.

In their responses, the school leaders demonstrated reflection and wisdom. They demonstrated that their mistakes have formed the leaders they are today.

For ease of reading, the responses are grouped into themes.

Get recruitment right

"A poor appointment - based too much on skills and not enough upon personal qualities - caused lasting and ongoing problems. When interviewing, I now require each candidate to convince me of their good character, rather than assuming that it's the case."

"I only hire people smarter than me"

But, while 'only hiring smart people reveals confidence and humility, it also suggests a narrow view of intelligence – i.e. smart equals intelligent. The best leaders recognise intelligence in all of its forms. You don't need to work with the smartest person in the room, you need to work with the person whose strengths are your weaknesses.

Be consistent, be clear and celebrate success

"Making exceptions - early in my career I made an exception for a child to participate in a football camp that was not open to their year group. When other parents found out I had a whole group in my office wanting to know why their children could not also participate. I am now extremely reluctant to make exceptions."

"I didn't celebrate all the work being done behind the scenes enough. Now I make a point of being consistent in celebrating our successes, no matter how small."

"I regretted not formalising my expectations, assuming conversations were adequate. Now I follow-up with written confirmation of what has been agreed. Or, at the very least, close meetings with a clear summary of who has agreed to do what."

Avoid micro-management

"Too closely of monitoring staff did cause me problems. There are often extenuating circumstances as to why teachers don't perform; over time, I developed a more understanding and caring attitude towards issues among teaching staff."

But, you can't do it alone

"I had to learn to coach staff and, even more importantly, delegate, so I didn't burn out!"

"I was promoted to a position where the previous incumbent had micro-managed. I made a commitment that I would prioritise servant leadership; I didn't want to add work to other school leaders and aimed to make their lives and work easier. However, in an effort to not encroach on their busy schedules I took on too much. As a result, and because I lacked the confidence (and desire) to delegate, we made far less progress than we should have."

"Working all night for weeks on end as a Housemaster and suffering illness as a result. Sleep is vital, you won't help anybody if you can't focus."

"Realizing that I alone could not secure the aspirations for my team and our students and that, in terms of leadership agility, as the Kenyan proverb has it: sticks in a bundle are unbreakable."

Though sometimes you will wish you had

"Being too friendly with staff and then losing respect as a leader."

"When I started out, it was safer and easier to make alliances with like-minded people. It led to some alienation of certain members of staff and blinded me to some of the issues with the people I was allied with. In my new post I have aimed for greater neutrality and it has paid dividends."

Trusting the wrong people.

"I overestimated my colleagues' loyalty; when their jobs were threatened they threw me under a bus. At the end of the day, on some matters you have to fight alone."

"I once thought that creating friendships at work was important when in fact it was detrimental."

Don't make assumptions

"Assuming new hires were settled when they needed more support. Now, I spend time and energy onboarding new hires, regardless of their level of experience."

Slow down, zoom out

"There are a number of mistakes I made that all would have benefited from not making decisions too quickly, or from seeking to impose myself too prematurely. I try to give things more time to play out these days."

"When I first moved into senior leadership, I was still so focused on the immediate instead of looking at the big picture. I had to learn to stop focusing on one class or team and begin to think of all the moving parts of a school."

"A number of times I have acted without getting as much of the big picture as I needed (or could have accessed)."

"Trying to teach too many (any) timetabled lessons - you are not always doing the students in your classes any favours."

"Don't make hot headed decisions."

"Saying yes to too many things and moving from one innovation to the next without giving time for the last to bed in."

"Missing one or two key details. Don't overlook small stuff."

Trust is hard earned, and easily lost

"I reacted to something I had been told by an adult, telling a child off without getting the full picture – and I made the wrong call. I now make sure I have a good understanding of all sides before I decide what response is appropriate."

"I broke a student's confidence once to her mother. It took months to get her trust back. Now I listen to people more and don't treat them as problems to solve."

Keep an eye on your own career

"Staying in one school too long. To avoid a fixed mindset, school leaders need to experience as many different ways of delivering education as possible. As Charles Darwin said:

"It is not the most intellectual of the species that survives; it is not the strongest that survives; but the species that survives is the one that is able to adapt to and to adjust best to the changing environment in which it finds itself."

"Walking away from the dream job because it was in the wrong country."

MYTHS
FALLACIES
FADS

WISDOM

MYTHS, FALACIES & FADS

"THE GREAT ENEMY OF THE TRUTH IS VERY OFTEN NOT THE LIE,
DELIBERATE, CONTRIVED AND DISHONEST, BUT THE MYTH,
PERSISTENT, PERSUASIVE AND UNREALISTIC." | **John F. Kennedy**

Your inbox is probably full of them.

Every day you probably receive e-mails, LinkedIn notifications or are bombarded by Facebook adverts proclaiming the latest educational topic du jour.

Some new technology is that latest breakthrough in #edtech, some new pedagogy the latest innovation in #nomoremarking, or some new website claims to be the latest solution to the #recruitmentcrisis.

Sorting the wheat from the chaff and the nonsense from the 'makes sense' can be challenging.

Over time school leaders develop increasingly sophisticated filters. They know what works, what has been tried before and what is just sales pitch. Wise school leaders remain open to new ideas, but they have developed systems and tools for identifying myths, fallacies and fads.

In the words of the Heads, some of the biggest myths, fallacies and fads in teaching and learning include:

"Unmitigated, feverish and blind belief in IT. The use of IT won't solve the issues facing education in the 21st century."

"That conventional teacher evaluation (pre-observation conference, full-lesson visit, lengthy write-up, and post-conference) actually improves teaching and learning."

"I don't believe that teachers should teach in one defined and dictated way. Just as pupils learn in many different ways, so teachers teach in many different ways. We should embrace this diversity, not quash it."

"That skills can replace knowledge entirely. We must have a depth of knowledge and understanding to be able to assess and judge. The two aspects are indivisible."

"Don't believe that every new study equals truth."

"Bring Your Own Device (BYOD) - Kids need to practice writing if exams stay pen to paper."

And, in school leadership generally:

"That the leader alone can fix things - only the team can do that."

"That the leader has all the power."

"The persistence of the myth of the messianic leader."

"Not sticking to your core beliefs and allowing fads and fashions to dictate development priorities always leads to lack of cohesion. Always keep the courage of your convictions whilst listening to those around you to sense-check decisions."

"Believing PD improves teaching and learning. A very weak correlation if any. Better hiring is the way to go."

"That educational leaders are experts."

"That leadership can be learnt from going on courses or reading books."

"For me you have to be very careful when employing consultants. In essence, they are sales people; often selling you and your school what you already know. So, use them wisely. Try to do as much as you can within the school and with your current resources. Only go outside when they really do add value."

"That all problems are solvable. Some are not."

"The belief that by hard work alone you can change a school for the better."

"That everyone is truly there due to their passion for student success – it was a sad day when I realised that this is not always true."

"That school leadership is lonely. It doesn't have to be."

"The belief that being young means you can't be experienced and vice versa."

WORK-LIFE BALANCE

"IMAGINE LIFE AS A GAME IN WHICH YOU ARE JUGGLING FIVE BALLS IN THE AIR. YOU NAME THEM — WORK, FAMILY, HEALTH, FRIENDS AND SPIRIT AND YOU'RE KEEPING ALL OF THESE IN THE AIR. YOU WILL SOON UNDERSTAND THAT WORK IS A RUBBER BALL. IF YOU DROP IT, IT WILL BOUNCE BACK. BUT THE OTHER FOUR BALLS — FAMILY, HEALTH, FRIENDS, AND SPIRIT — ARE MADE OF GLASS. IF YOU DROP ONE OF THESE, THEY WILL BE IRREVOCABLY SCUFFED, MARKED, NICKED, DAMAGED, OR EVEN SHATTERED. THEY WILL NEVER BE THE SAME. YOU MUST UNDERSTAND THAT AND STRIVE FOR BALANCE IN YOUR LIFE." | **Brian Dyson,** former vice chairman and COO of Coca-Cola

Teaching is a deeply rewarding profession.

It is also stressful.

You will know the statistics. You probably have friends who are the statistics. Study after study reports high rates of turnover, absenteeism and teacher shortages. In the US, about 260,000 teachers leave the profession annually, most for reasons other than retirement. In the UK, nearly a third of new teachers leave the profession within three years, often citing poor wellbeing as the reason.

Teaching is tough; so is school leadership.

Despite the metronomic routines of a career lived to timetable, you can never guarantee what each day will bring. So much cannot be anticipated. Addressing unforeseen problems, numerous crises, and perpetual student (and staff) disagreements seems to accelerate time – 'free' periods disappear, like tears in rain. The very nature of schooling works against a sense of achievement and lengthens to-do lists. Evenings and weekends spent marking, report-writing, doing paperwork and, these days, managing emails, eat into your home life and your social life.

I talk to teachers and school leaders every day. They share their thoughts publicly and privately;

some in my classes or in the comments sections on group forums, some in private emails. Many are struggling. Some are engaged in a healthy struggle, the 'good stress' of working at a challenging job. Others are frazzled. They leave school each day, and when the marking is done, their own kids fed and put to bed, they collapse. They survive school days fuelled by coffee and desperation. Many are thinking seriously about leaving the profession.

When we rush through our days, we miss the numerous joys of teaching: the boundless variety of young people; the passion that we feel and share for our subjects; the gratitude for colleagues who fuel our spirits every day.

We forget to smile and gather perspective.

We forget that teaching is the best job in the world.

To offer some help I asked whether the school leaders I surveyed had any tips for maintaining (some degree of) work-life balance.

Let's get the depressing responses out of the way first:

"The only way I've been able to manage work-life balance, is to accept that there isn't a worklife balance."

"No - I want to exhaust myself in the work."

"There's a life, and work takes up a huge portion of it."

"No tips I am afraid; I have never found a way of getting a balance!"

"Mmm. Please can you let me have the answers to this!"

Now, to the more positive:

"Get a dog."

"Don't battle against unrealistic expectations of a work-life balance: work hard during term time, relax in the holidays. Have other outlets for when you are not working: writing, music, fitness, whatever relaxes you."

"Get up early."

"Triage everything - does it need to be done now and by me?"

"Don't run around trying to solve every single small problem in a school. Empower others. Your time is important and if you are spending all of it fixing other people's problems you are implicitly suggesting that your work/time is less important."

"It's only a job and should remain as such."

On having a social life:

"Foster relationships outside-of-school, with people who have nothing to do with education!"

On exercise:

"Run."

"Regular walks to clear the mind."

"Try to find time every day to exercise. This need only be 20 minutes and is difficult to discipline yourself. However, exercise first thing in the morning sets you up for the day. Exercise after work, refreshes you before you tackle your next task; better than automatically reaching for a gin and tonic after work!"

"For me, exercising first thing in the morning helps."

"Exercise three times a week."

On protecting personal time:

"Learn to say no - and mean it."

"Draw the line - work is work (including the evening events) and home is home. Period."

"Establish a time at which you will not ever (ever, ever) check school emails."

"Have a cut-off for school work. Separate work apps from leisure devices."

"Work hard throughout the day, through your breaks if necessary and into the early evening, but do not take work with you when you leave the threshold of the school grounds."

"I don't send work related e-mails after work (I do draft them though)."

"Take an invisible bag. Put all your worries inside it when you enter your house. Completely switch off your phone when sitting for dinner with family."

"No electronic devices during meals, no correspondence or work after 8pm. An educational emergency is an extreme rarity - it can wait until tomorrow."

"I try to do something for 'me' every day. That could be exercise, getting a haircut, watching some sports highlights. I find that just labelling it as my time, whether long or short, makes me feel I have put myself first at least once in the day."

"You can have family, friends, life and a senior management position. When my son is playing football or my daughter is playing her sax in a concert, this is a priority above all others!"

"I try to keep Sundays free for the family. However, if there is work needed doing, and there undoubtedly is, I'll spread the load over the mornings, keeping the afternoons and evenings free."

"It doesn't always work but I aim to have the weekend free of meetings, email and such. Of course, there are weekend events but if you are passionate about education they shouldn't feel like work."

"Make time to get out and live life every weekend. Otherwise the job will consume you."

"Allow weekends for family time."

GO TO INTERVIEW
QUESTIONS

"EXPERIENCE IS NOT WHAT HAPPENS TO [US]. IT IS WHAT [WE DO]
WITH WHAT HAPPENS TO [US]." | **Aldous Huxley** [adapted]

Who are more important, the students or the staff? Which is more important, learning or teaching? If you saw a senior student getting into a car with a respected colleague, what would you do? Describe your worst day as a teacher.

Perhaps more than any other, responses to the 'go to' interview question are testament to the variety of skills required of teachers and school leaders.

From providing pastoral care to pedagogical expertise, from putting out chairs in assembly to deciding how many chairs to purchase, from counselling students to consoling staff, working in a school is tough – and so too is the interview process.

The Heads surveyed were asked to reflect on their favourite interview questions.

What questions do they always ask? Or, which questions do they turn to if they need to spice an interview up. Their responses make interesting reading and will, hopefully, be useful to you when you face a wise Head, or a panel of wisened recruiters, at interview.

In a few cases the responses came with additional commentary, we'll start with those:

Why do you want to work at [school name]?

COMMENTARY: An obvious one and, really, that's the point. I ask this early on as a filter. Candidates should expect some variant of this question and should be prepared for it; if they don't it is highly unlikely they are the kind of teacher/leader I want to appoint. The advice: do your research on the school!

Tell me about a successful classroom management strategy you have embedded in your lessons.

COMMENTARY: Again, perhaps obvious. The kicker though is in the word 'embedded', and it is that element I would probe further. I want to know that the candidate has reflected on their pedagogy and has developed, and continually refined, a 'toolbox' of approaches. I want to know about *strategies*, not just one-off incidents.

Why do we teach [insert subject] in schools?

COMMENTARY: A great left-field question, especially if you don't ask them about their subject/ specialism. Ask a Maths teacher why we teach Drama, or a Drama teacher why we teach Physics and watch them try to think outside of their own subject silo. The answers can reveal volumes about the value a candidate places on education in general, not just the value they place on their subject.

If you overheard some students talking about you, what would they likely be saying?

COMMENTARY: I was asked this myself a few years back, but in the form of colleagues doing the talking. When I became a Head I adopted the question but changed it to students. I find that asking what students might say prompts more critical responses. We generally hope that our colleagues will say nice things about us, we are less hopeful when it is students. This helps to reveal reflexivity, self-awareness, humility and any sense of ego.

Other responses came without commentary, but provide a useful list of 'go to' questions.

Some questions are obvious:

"Why did you choose education over all other options?"

"Tell us about yourself."

"Who was your favorite teacher and why?"

"Analyse the best lesson that you have taught. What made it great?"

"What is the best quality a teacher should have?"

"At what time in your life did you decide to become a teacher?"

"How have you recently developed/changed your pedagogy?"

"What would it look/sound/feel like in your classroom if I walked in?"

"What is the greatest personal (non-school based) challenge you have faced?"

"I am always interested in candidates' hobbies, you can tell a lot about a character and a teacher from their outside experiences."

Others are more challenging:

"What is the most recent education book or article you've read and how did it affect your thinking?

"What three words would your senior colleagues use to describe you? What three words would your students in your school say best described you?"

"What is the most difficult part of being a teacher and how is that different from my next question, which is: which aspect of teaching would you not miss at all?"

"To what extent are you comfortable moving the onus of responsibility and control of learning away from yourself and towards students?"

"'Can you give me an example of constructive feedback and how you responded to it?' (I want to know that I can honestly and constructively talk about the issues that arise with my teachers)."

"What would your worst student say about you? Then, what would your best student say about you?"

"Casting yourself forward, a year from now, and with three full terms in post behind you, what positive differences have you made and what might you have not got quite right?"

"I've got a number of 'go to' questions that I find can be incredibly revealing. Perhaps my favourite is: 'If you don't get this job, what will the main reason be?'"

"'Has your teaching ever been evaluated?' Responses and reactions continue to vary from one of surprise and short answers to in-depth explanations and very interesting opinions on the subject."

"What is the thing you are most proud of, to date, in your career?"

Some are eclectic:

"If you were a Disney character - which one would you be and why?"

"How we perceive ourselves it not always how others perceive us. How do you think the way people perceive you is different to the way you perceive yourself?"

"If you entered [insert name of appropriate TV talent show], what song would you sing or what would be your unique talent?"

"If you were a box of cereal, what would you be and why?"

"You're a new addition to the crayon box, what color would you be and why?

"What was the last gift you gave someone?"

"Are you more of a hunter or a gatherer?"

"What is your least favorite thing about humanity?"

Others were focused on aspiring leaders:

"How do you coach, supervise, and evaluate your teachers?"

"After, say, five years in post, how will the school be different as a result of your leadership?"

"What do you believe is the most important skill you need as a school leader?"

"As a leader how would you contribute to the wellbeing of your staff?"

"What keeps you awake at night?"

"In what different ways would you manage a young and a veteran member of your staff?"

And, two final thoughts:

"I always allow space for candidates to ask me questions - it often tells me more than the answers they have prepared to my questions."

"If we decided not to appoint you, what would we be missing out on?"

COMMENTARY: A final chance for the candidate to sell themselves and to tell us anything important we might not have picked up on.

QUOTES TO
LEAD BY

"A FINE QUOTATION IS A DIAMOND IN THE HAND OF A MAN OF WIT AND A PEBBLE IN THE HAND OF A FOOL." | **Joseph Roux**

As teachers we tend to love quotes. We use them in lessons. We decorate classrooms and corridors with them. We base assemblies around them.

As you will probably have experienced, school leaders often have a 'bank' of quotes they like to use. You know, the ones that are parroted, satirised and subverted in the staffroom.

But, leaders adopt and use quotes for a purpose.

Quotes give us voice when our own words fail us. Quotes provide a springboard for thoughts, arguments and debates. Quotes can summarise and encapsulate discussion, providing punctuation, levity or insight.

Quotes can be, and often are, over used. But, the wise Head knows when a quote is appropriate. Here are some favourites.

Quotes from the school leaders themselves:

"It's all about the students."

"Put yourself in the shoes of the students."

"Ask three questions of any decision. Firstly, does it help learning? Secondly, does it impact on safety? Finally, is it within budget? Always in that order."

"If a school rule can't be justified and explained, it shouldn't be a school rule."

"Teachers teach the way they were taught, unless they have effective professional development."

"Get up, dress up, turn up."

"You're only as good as those you lead."

"Walk the talk; you are being watched all the time."

"Don't look back, you ain't going that way."

"What is more effective, one person saying the same thing a 1,000 times or a 1,000 people saying the same thing once?"

"Whenever you face difficulty, that this is the time to shine. Difficulty is a disguised blessing for school leaders if faced positively."

"It's often easier to ask for forgiveness rather than permission."

"Enjoy the experience."

Quotes by educational thinkers, researchers and philosophers:

From one wise Head: "There are so many! Here are the first three that spring to mind":

"Perfect is the enemy of good" ~*Voltaire*

COMMENTARY: We can often undo much excellence in the pursuit of perfection.

"The rock in the river is the river - a reminder that the difficulties in the journey is an important part of that journey."

"And let that be a lesson to you all. Nobody beats Vitas Gerulaitis 17 times in a row."

COMMENTARY: After beating Jimmy Connors at the January 1980 Masters; Gerulaitis had lost their previous 16 matches."

"The task of education is not to teach subjects: it is to teach students." ~*Ken Robinson, Out of Our Minds.*

"The fundamental work of a school leader is simple: engender and sustain the best possible environment for teaching and learning... Hire the best teachers you can find, support them in every way possible, help them grow, evaluate them fairly, set and exemplify high expectations for everyone, and create and insist on a climate and culture where students feel safe, known, and challenged. That's the only vision a Principal needs." *~John Ritchie (2013)*

"Accept the things you cannot change; have the courage to change the things that need to be changed, however unpopular, and have the wisdom to know the difference."

"As teachers we are in a unique position to offer to our students not just our capacity to impart knowledge and skills, but our essence as people". *~Daniel Siegel, The Mindful Brain (2007)*

Famous quotes, by famous people:

"Knowledge speaks but wisdom listens." *~Jimi Hendrix*

"If you put your mind to it, you can accomplish anything." *~Doc Brown, Back to the Future (1985)*

"I have the power to create or destroy." *~Hein Ginott*

"The gardener does not make a plant grow. The job of a gardener is to create optimal conditions for growth." *~Robinson*

"The more expertise and experience people gain, the more entrenched they become in the way they view things. We become prisoners of our prototypes." *~Eric Dane*

"A desk is a dangerous place from which to view the world." *~John le Carre*

"All models are wrong, but some are useful." *~George EP Box*

> "BUT THOSE WHO HOPE IN THE LORD WILL RENEW THEIR STRENGTH. THEY WILL SOAR ON WINGS LIKE EAGLES; THEY WILL RUN AND NOT GROW WEARY, THEY WILL WALK AND NOT BE FAINT."

Isaiah 40:31

And, one contra view:

"I really don't like quotes. If I hear Gandhi again I think I will cry. Talking is not always the best leadership facet. Listening, I believe, is far better."

INTERESTING ANECDOTES AND STORIES

"NEVER LET YOUR SENSE OF MORALS PREVENT YOU FROM DOING WHAT IS RIGHT." | **Isaac Asimov,** Foundation (1942)

Storytelling is the oldest of all the arts.

Since the dawn of humankind we have told stories. Still to this day, we sit around campfires and tell stories.

Stories entertain and they guide. We use stories to escape and we use them as instruction manuals. We tell stories as a gift to future generations. Stories connect the past and present to the future. Stories are a means of passing on wisdom.

I didn't expect the school leaders to have time to share lengthy stories, certainly not via an online survey. I asked for anecdotes that capture the essence of stories they tell about school leadership; vignettes about the challenges and joys, highs and lows of school leadership.

Let's get the lows out of the way:

"When teachers think only of themselves, not their colleagues or students, and are incapable of changing or improving."

"Being suspended from my school, sacked and then winning unjustified dismissal, and still not being reinstated. It has changed me forever."

"The difficulty seeing visible improvements from initiatives introduced."

"Problems forming new teams that get results and do so with thorough professionalism."

But, there were also plenty of highs:

"Hearing from a former teacher what he has become a Head because of me."

"Getting into classrooms and seeing wonderful learning moments taking place."

"A student came to my office the other day, he doesn't have a dad in his life, and wanted advice about going to meet his girlfriend's parents for dinner for the first time. I felt like I must be doing something right if a high school kid would ask advice on a matter so personal even when I'm the Principal. I hope I can continue to protect that fine balance. For the record, I told him it was okay to bring a bottle of wine, but not okay to drink it! Also, to leave the Slayer t-shirt at home."

"Every once in a while an alumnus will tell you how much you influenced them. It will come when you least expect it and when you need to hear it."

"Unity. I take great pleasure from seeing a happy, performing team"

"I was principal of a large school in Papua New Guinea. The staff were all nationals. I was there for 6 years. When I arrived the school was in a poor condition - the physical structures, the staff morale and the finances. We achieved a lot during those 6 years. The pivotal point was when the old library burnt down. The staff were devastated. I just saw a glorious opportunity given the size of the insurance policy. The new facility created a resurgence of community pride in the school. The new opportunities created by the new resources opened the school to new directions. Sometimes an apparent disaster turns into a blessing of unexpected fortune."

RESOURCES

"TO ACQUIRE KNOWLEDGE, ONE MUST STUDY; BUT TO ACQUIRE
WISDOM, ONE MUST OBSERVE." | **Marilyn vos Savant**

As an aspiring leader, what should you invest in? Where should you be spending your time and money?

You need, of course, to be developing yourself professionally: attending conferences, attaining higher level degrees, consciously honing your instructional leadership capacities.

But, what else should you invest in? Are there useful resources a school leader should own, develop, acquire or cultivate?

The school leaders I sampled offered these thoughts:

"Follow Teacher's Toolkit on Twitter"

"Get subscriptions to the *Times Educational Supplement*, *Schools Week*, and a good newspaper. Carve out time to read them."

"Subscribe to '*The Marshall Memo*' - a weekly summary of research and ideas from 60 publications." [Note: This came up on multiple occasions and is well worth the subscription price]

"Get two mobile phones; keep one for school use only…your sanity will thank you"

"Join an ongoing leadership programme, such as a *Masters in Educational Leadership* or equivalent. In my own experience, deep reflection upon the process of leadership and/or management is never a pressing priority and this helps to raise it up the list."

"The PTC is very useful. Having access to a large email list is an asset when working on new ideas and looking for benchmark data and ideas."

"Get some fun ties and bright socks; it's a school after all, not a bank."

"Spend some money on a decent laptop. Better still, spend the school's money on a decent laptop. The time and frustration saved will pay huge dividends…especially when it comes to late night working!"

"Get copies of Ken Blanchard and Toby Travis books." [Note: A quick Google or Amazon search will return plenty of relevant books by both authors]

"As a school leader, you need to look smart and professional - invest in a good suit but not one that makes you look 65 years old (unless you are 65 years old)! People do judge by appearances, find time to invest in yourself and your appearance."

"A stock of high-quality shirts (pink preferred)."

"An online calendar accessible by all staff - essential to organising the many facets of school life."

"A journal that you carry around with you - eventually you will be in a hallway or a boardroom without a computer or phone and someone will ask you for something and you'll say no problem and then you'll forget to email - WRITE IT DOWN!"

"The ASCL annual conference has always been an excellent way to recharge my enthusiasm and to reflect upon the challenges schools face and how we can find solutions together."

"Invest in your PA, they are vital."

"An office library. And make sure you know how to account for your books, but having a conversation about a new concept or topic and then putting that into the hands of a stakeholder or colleague is a great way to connect and spread ideas."

"Teaching materials must take precedence! Other than that, funding for outings and time for teacher team building exercises."

Plus, a few very practical ideas:

"A gym subscription."

"A GPS running watch such as a Garmin to track daily movement (avoiding too long without a walkabout) but also encouraging exercise at other times."

"Good health, exercise, healthy eating and meditation."

"A room with a view."

"A toilet you can escape to without being seen!"

BOOKS TO READ

"The more that you READ, the more things you will KNOW.
The more that you LEARN, the more places you'll GO."
Dr. Seuss

We encourage children to do it, but how often do we do it ourselves?

As teachers and school leaders we read. We read a lot. But, how often do we read for ourselves? How often do we read for pleasure?

Fiction or non-fiction, what was the last book you read? More to the point, what was the last book you read with purpose? A book you deliberately chose, actively sought out and devoured.

We know reading is important, but do we devote enough time to it? Many of us do, but not all. And we should.

Mark Manson, an author and prolific reader, quotes his high school English teacher as saying "We read books because we can never know enough people." It's one of those pithy truths we underappreciate. We tend to self-select the people in our lives; our friendship groups reflect our shared interests, our views and our experiences. We tend to prefer the company of people who confirm our previously held beliefs.

Reading breaks us out of this circle.

Reading takes us outside of our own narrow experience and frame of reference.

Books expand our experiences far beyond their natural reach; they transport us into the brains of the author. It's through books that we glimpse the experiences of others. Reading exercises our empathic muscles — it teaches us to see the world as others do, to understand their views and perspectives, even if we don't necessarily agree with them or like them.

But the cognitive benefits of reading go far beyond empathy. It increases our ability to communicate, our ability to reason, our creativity, and our ability to see connections between events.

Watching TV makes you passive; social media makes you susceptible to suggestion. You are simply an empty vessel receiving noise. Music, while engaging, is abstract and formless and often occupies the background of our mind, not the contents of it. Reading, in contrast, is like doing bench presses for the mind.

To help you put in some reading reps, I asked for book recommendations. Review the list below, choose a book that interests you and let it lead you to another…and another. And then when you come to a dead end, come back to the list and start again.

Education-specific books

Books by Ken Robinson:*

1. **Creative Schools:**
   "Any of his books make worthwhile reading and his TED Talks are pretty much compulsory viewing for any educationalist]

2. **Out of our minds**

Books by John Hattie:*

1. **Visible Learning:**
   "Or anything else John Hattie has written; his website has plenty of useful information."

Books by Dylan William:*

1. **Inside the Black Box:**
   "A seminal text. Changed the way we think about assessment"

2. **Making Good Progress**

3. **Creating the Schools our Children Needs**

- **The New Meaning of Educational Change** by Michael Fullan
  "The number of editions and reprints is testimony to its influence"

- **Teach Like a Champion 2.0** by Doug Lemov

- **Transforming Schools** by John M Anderson and Miranda Jeffers

- **A Desolation of Learning & The Courage to Teach** by Chris Woodhead
  "Love him or loathe him."

- **To Know as We are Known** by Parker Palmer

- **Democracy and Education/Experience and Education** by John Dewey

- **World Class: tackling the ten biggest challenges facing schools today** by David James and Ian Warwick

- **Qualities of Effective Principals** by James Stronge, Holly Richard, and Nancy Catano

- **Culture Counts: changing relations in education** by Russell Bishop and Ted Glynn

- **The Challenges of Educational Leadership** by Mike Bottery

"Heavy on the theory, but very useful for anyone doing Doctoral level study"

- **Clever Lands** by Lucy Crehan
  "One women's tale of a round the world educational adventure. She visited schools, and lived with teachers, in five countries. Essential reading for international school teachers."

Business Books

- **Good to Great** by Jim Collins
  "This book had a huge impact on my approaches to leadership."

- **7 Habits of Highly effective People** by Stephen Covey

- **Wherever You Go, There You Are** by Jon Kabat-Zinn
  "Insightful guidance on being able to thrive, rather than simply survive, in leadership roles."

- **Originals** by Adam Grant

- **Our Iceberg is Melting** by John Kotter

- **CEO Capital: A Guide to Building CEO Reputation and Company Success** by Leslie Gaines-Ross

- **Thinking Fast and Slow** by Daniel Kahneman

- **Outliers: The Story of Success** by Malcolm Gladwell
- "Worth the price for the chapter on the effects of age relative to academic year cut-off dates alone."

- **The Age of the Paradox** by Charles Handy

General Comments/Recommendations

"The 'First 90 Days' by Michael D. Watkins has an excellent chapter about the different leadership challenges we face. It reinforced to me how important it is to identify what the specific needs of a leadership role are and how adaptive you may need to be as a result, rather than acting in the same way as in previous roles."

"Anything by John Tomsett and also his blog. John West Burnman's books are also very good."

"Too many to mention but Andy Hargreaves 'Sustainable leadership' I particularly enjoyed, especially the first chapter."

"No one book; educational leadership has so many areas to cover."

"I would recommend a broad list encompassing many different views of leadership. Alex Ferguson's autobiography has stood out, of late."

* John Hattie, Ken Robinson and Dylan William were mentioned by numerous contributors. These books are worthy of reading if only to be able to join the conversation.

DON'T BE A HERO

"WHAT MAKES SUPERMAN A HERO IS NOT THAT HE HAS
POWER, BUT THAT HE HAS THE WISDOM AND THE MATURITY
TO USE THE POWER WISELY." | **Christopher Reeve**

Does school leadership really matter?

The reassuring answer is yes it does, but it has to be the right type of leadership.

When most of us think of leadership, we think of one person doing something to another person. This is 'influence'; a leader who has the power, authority or capacity to *influence* others. The word 'leader' conjures up visions of a striking figure on a rearing white horse crying "Follow me!" Words like 'charismatic' and 'heroic' are common.

But is this heroic figure the most appropriate image for today's school leaders?

No. In contemporary schools, the most appropriate leader is one who can lead others to lead themselves.

We know from John Hattie's work on visible learning (2009), for example, that leaders actually have less influence – yes, <u>less</u> – on student achievement than other factors (teacher quality for example).

The best leaders then are the ones who get the best out of teachers.

In fact, some leadership approaches are so ineffective that, if adopted, leaders may as well stay at home. Consider the difference between transformational and instructional leadership.

Transformational leaders set a vision, inspiring goals for the school, energise staff, protect teachers from external demands and give them high levels of autonomy in the classroom. Instructional leaders focus on classroom observations. They build the collective professional trust needed to enable teachers to conduct peer observations. They ensure that teachers receive professional development opportunities which enhance student learning. They align all aspects of the school environment in a manner conducive to learning.

The impact of these different styles? Hattie's research found that instructional leadership is far more effective. For the data nerds: the average effect size from transformational leadership was .11, whereas the impact of instructional leadership was .42 (Hattie, 2009). That's like the difference in acceleration speed between a Ferrari and a Ford.

What sets these two styles apart? One is focused on the leader as the agent and energy behind transformation, the other is focused on the engine of change itself – learning – and on all of its component parts. Instructional leadership transcends the notion of leaders as heroes, focusing instead on leaders as *hero-makers*.

The spotlight then should be on achievements of the followers, not the leader. Improving student outcomes requires a team of teachers, students, parents and community members all working in collaboration.

The message is clear: excellence is achievable, but only if leaders are dedicated to tapping the vast potential within each individual.

Most of all, this does not mean that transformational leaders are needed to influence followers to comply with and carry out the vision of the heroic leader. Rather, the vision itself needs to reflect and draw upon the vast resources contained within individuals.

Perhaps this spirit was captured most succinctly by Lao-tzu, a sixth-century B.C. Chinese philosopher, when he wrote the following:

> A LEADER IS BEST WHEN PEOPLE BARELY KNOW HE EXISTS,
> NOT SO GOOD WHEN PEOPLE OBEY AND ACCLAIM HIM.
> WORSE WHEN THEY DESPISE HIM.
> BUT OF A GOOD LEADER, WHO TALKS LITTLE,
> WHEN HIS WORK, IS DONE, HIS AIM FULFILLED,
> THEY WILL SAY: WE DID IT OURSELVES.
>
> **IN OTHER WORDS, DON'T BE A HERO.**

REFERENCE

Hattie, John. (2008). Visible Learning. Abingdon, Oxon: Routledge

DON'T CHASE
FALSE LEGACIES

"WHAT WE DO IN LIFE, ECHOES IN ETERNITY."
Maximus Decimus Meridius

The quote, made famous by the movie *Gladiator*, is from Maximus Decimus Meridius.

It's a powerful, inspiring line.

But, far too many people - especially leaders - do themselves and those they serve little justice by 'performing for history', or, at least for their own history.

The best leaders do the right thing, today, because it's the right thing. They pursue excellence because excellence is intrinsically valuable, not because they want to be admired.

How many leaders do you know though who are obsessed with their own image/reputation/paycheck/workflow/group of cronies (delete as applicable)? Or, how many play things safe, not wanting to take risks that could turn out badly...at the expense of possible opportunities they'll never even know they missed.

Forget echoing in eternity—just speak loudly enough to be heard right now.

Or better yet, let today's actions do the talking. Your legacy will be a combination of actions made in service of progress today, improvement made now, and for others, not for your own (future) image.

This doesn't mean taking a short-termist approach, it means not letting worries about the echoes of eternity affect making the right decision today.

TYPE TYPE TYPE TYPE TYPE TYPE TY-
PE TYPE TYPE TYPE TYPE TYPE TYPE
TYPE TYPE TYPE TYPE TYPE TYPE TY-
PE TYPE TYPE TYPE TYPE TYPE TYPE

WHAT TYPE ARE YOU?

"KNOWING YOURSELF IS THE BEGINNING OF ALL WISDOM." | **Aristotle**

> "THERE ARE TEACHERS THAT I HAVE LET GO,
> NOT BECAUSE THEY'RE NOT GOOD, THEY
> JUST DON'T FIT THE CONTEXT. I EXPLAIN THAT
> IT IS CLIENTS WHO ARE PAYING YOUR WAGES;
> SOME TEACHERS DON'T GET IT."

These are the words of a school Head. Not a CEO, a Bursar or Business Manager, a Head. A Head who happily refers to parents as clients. Admittedly, he runs a fee-paying school, but the word 'client' is still jarring.

Yet, this type of language is echoing out of boardrooms, down corridors and into classrooms. Education, we are repeatedly told, is big business. School leaders are expected to balance the aims of educational and financial effectiveness. The bottom line, for many Heads, is that the bottom-line matters.

This presents an uneasy paradox.

School leaders must balance the aims of educational and financial effectiveness. How does the born and bred educationalist cope in this environment?

The response to this question was the focus of research interviews with Head of schools, small and large, profit and not-for-profit, public and private. The result was a range of Headship 'types.'

You may recognise yourself (or your school's Head) amongst them.

The Teacher-Head

Teacher-Heads identify as practitioners. Management demands are seen as functional requirements of the job, necessary but incidental.  For this Head, it is education that is emotionally fulfilling:

TEACHER-HEAD

"I want to be in the classrooms, talking to the kids, talking to teachers; being out there, not in the office."

The Head-Teacher

Head-Teacher's see themselves slightly differently; the reversal of the nouns is significant. The Head-Teacher understands that a Head is not only a teacher but also Head of the teachers (a manager).

HEAD-TEACHER

These Heads remain committed to education but recognise that leadership shifts them away from teaching and towards management. To an extent they accept this, but they still want to be "one of them" - a Head, but a teacher too.

The Pragmatist-Broker

For the Pragmatist-Broker, being a Head is about doing whatever it takes to support school improvement. They are willing to get "their hands dirty in the
business stuff"; they see themselves as educationalists but accept that management thinking can offer pragmatic benefit. As one Head put it:

"I am focused on the educational well-being of the young people in my care but the business context provides a really excellent discipline for what I do."

The Educational Manager

The Educational Manager goes one step further. Affinity with education remains, but these Heads embrace their manage-
ment responsibilities:

"Without the business perspective, we are missing huge elements of a school's potential.

So, you really do need to blend the two. I bring that blend."

For these Heads, management responsibilities are no longer incidental; they are managers of education - a subtle, but significant shift.

The Educational Executive

The Educational Executive sees education and management as complimentary. For this Head, effective management is just as important as  effective education. Efficiency, productivity, accountability, and, in some contexts, profit, all matter. These Heads have come to see management (including non-educational tasks) as part of the job – an entirely natural, desirable and welcomed part of leading a school.

EDUCATIONAL EXECUTIVE

As the types show, today's school leaders must demonstrate abilities beyond just 'instructional leadership'. Just as important as pedagogical preparation is the ability/willingness to undertake managerial tasks. In other words, the contemporary school leader must be a HYBRID.

Hybridity is a powerful concept. Hybridity – blending instructional leadership and management – enables Heads to maintain legitimacy as educators while also undertaking tasks that are not directly educational. In other words, a Hybrid can successfully be a manager and still be considered (and still consider themselves) a professional educator; they can enjoy spreadsheets, metrics and data, identifying with performance while still being a passionate pedagogue.

As Dr Stephen Whitehead puts it:

> "...THE HYBRID PROFESSIONAL DOES NOT OCCUPY A SINGULAR PROFESSIONAL IDENTITY BUT HAS THE EMOTIONAL INTELLIGENCE AND COGNITIVE FLEXIBILITY TO MOVE BETWEEN IDENTITIES, AND ORGANISA-TIONAL DEMANDS, SITUATIONALLY; E.G. THEY ARE CONTINUALLY IN FLUX AND NOT DEVOTED TO A SINGULAR WAY OF BEING A LEADER. THIS MEANS THEY CAN DEVELOP A WIDER REPERTOIRE OF RESPONSES TO LEADERSHIP DILEMMAS AND, IMPORTANTLY, ARE NOT AFRAID TO DO SO."

Being comfortable as a hybrid helps Heads navigate the uncertainty and ambiguity of what Headship (now) is and what Heads (now) must be able to do.

How then does one develop hybridity? My research suggests the following:

Acquire management training – MBAs may not currently be required for Headship positions, but they do seem to facilitate hybridity, or at least openness to new forms of managerial identification. Choosing to undertake an MBA (or similar) would therefore be an important first step towards hybridity. Further, the skills and knowledge gained through management training will add at a practical level to your ability to perform the occupational requirements of management.

Acquire Experience in a 'corporate' school environment – Experience in a corporate school environment is likely to demand the adoption and acceptance of hybrid practices. Paradoxically, this context need not be for-profit or commercially owned - many not-for-profit schools are run on equally corporate lines – it simply needs to expose you to 'corporate' demands.

Reflect on the purpose of school leadership – For some, this purpose will be an enhancement of social good, student well-being and service-led values; others will be more at ease with the Darwinian reality of for-profit education. Those positions, in many schools, are not mutually exclusive, but reflecting on whether you are comfortable at the extremes of the latter is essential when picking your way through the daily demands of school leadership.

Develop adaptability and resilience – Hybridity demands adaptability and resilience; the successful hybrid will thrive amongst, not suffer, the slings and arrows of increasingly complex school environments.

Develop emotional intelligence – The successful leader must be sensitive to the needs of the teachers, technicians, carers and cared-for in their charge. Hard-headed, autocratic, paternalistic and masculine approaches have no place in the modern school. Moreover, whereas *you* may have the pliability, strength and resilience to accept, and indeed thrive in plural environments, you need the emotional intelligence to recognise that those they manage may not share the same openness – and, indeed, may feel very vulnerable working under those very conditions.

In short, if such a thing as the pure educationalist ever existed (a doubtful claim), then those days are long gone. Contemporary school leaders are required to operate effectively across (potentially) contradictory positions; they must be both practitioner and manager. It may be uncomfortable to sit on the fulcrum of this duality, but contemporary school leadership requires hybridity:

> "I WANT THE CHALK DUST UNDER THE FINGERNAILS, AND I THRIVE IN THAT, BUT IF THAT'S ALL I WAS DOING, I MIGHT NOT GET THE SAME SORT OF CHALLENGE FROM THE MANAGEMENT STUFF."

Instead then of education being replaced or degraded by management, instead of the educationalist bemoaning the 'business of education', what hybridity offers is a new view of school leadership – as hybrid.

Are you a hybrid?

FINAL WORDS

"WE ARE MADE WISE NOT BY THE RECOLLECTION OF OUR PAST,
BUT BY THE RESPONSIBILITY FOR OUR FUTURE."
George Bernard Shaw

It seems apt that the closing words go to the wise Heads.

Take these comments as their parting wisdom; their sage guidance as you progress your leadership career, their final encouragement on your journey.

May their wisdom make you a wise Head.

"Have a plan: do you want to go the pastoral route, or the academic route? What skills do you need to develop early on? Take external advice from those outside the organisation."

"Learn as much as you can about as much as you can! Keep sharpening your tools."

"Work as a team. There is golden information in every staff room and it is a leader's job to dig for it."

"Never be too busy for anyone. As a school leader, people come first so you have to find time to talk, meet or support them. They will trust you first and your message second, so spend time building relationships and being interested in staff as people. Be prepared to be self-effacing but at the same time make sure that high profile tasks are completed. Plan for meetings and presentations as word travels fast when these go well. You are always shaping the values of the school so take every chance to reinforce them. If you aren't addressing behaviour, uniform or staff conflict, it is harder to expect others to do the same. Base every decision on purpose: ask what do we believe, why do we believe it and as result what will we do every day in our school?"

"Know who you are and what you believe in. The school business is a people and relationship business... not just about systems."

"Get to know your staff. Attend staff social functions, but leave early."

"Shift the conversation to results. While not evaluating teachers on test scores (a truly bad idea), always be talking in a low-stakes way about whether teaching is getting measurable results. This can take place after short classroom visits, talking to teacher teams about exit tickets, quizzes, and tests, and in more formal end-of-year value-added reports from teams."

"As John Hattie says, 'Know thy impact!' Reflection is key. Why are you doing what you are doing? Ensure you find a good coach/mentor/sage who can counsel and encourage and be aware that there will be many times when you will need to replenish your own reservoirs of resilience."

"Be authentic and all else follows."

"Promote and facilitate classroom management techniques and strategies to increase every educators time to teach."

"You will be a better leader for taking time out sometimes. When you are working, give it everything but you must take time to refuel."

"It is possible to have children and then return to the workplace in a senior position. Trusting your senior team is crucial - trust your judgement in these people and let them manage."

"As a woman in a female dominated vocation, it can be difficult at the top. Surround yourself with people who you trust and are in the job for the right reasons."

"Question norms. If someone says 'it's traditional', question it."

"Learn when to say no. Not every offer is worth chasing, and sometimes you need to think in terms of returns on your time."

"The best leaders are those that have doubted and questioned their ability to lead in sufficient depth. Humility, self-awareness, a genuine passion for education and focus on serving the entire school community are of paramount importance. If you have these elements then quell the doubts and take the lead."

"Enjoy it and take the time to mix with the students and spend time with them as this will help you when things get busy and stressful."

"Remember it is the relationships you develop with students that is the most important part of your leadership role. Your students don't have to like you, but you do have to win their respect."

"Read widely, keep up to speed with local and global changes in education, don't sit back and wait for things to be done to you (go out there and take every opportunity to be a pioneer)."

"Praise your staff as often as possible."

"Do not entertain gossip and egos."

"Not everything needs to be fixed. Some situations fix themselves and, just as educators we challenge students, sometimes, as leaders, we need to challenge teachers to fix their own problems in their own way."

"Don't be afraid to be creative or innovative. Don't be afraid of the emotional."

"Be yourself. Go for it - make a difference."

LIST OF CONTRIBUTORS

I offer my thanks to the school leaders whose wisdom, stories, advice and lessons are the essence of this book. A few of these contributors are named below, other wished to remain anonymous. My thanks and gratitude goes to all of those who took the time to share their wisdom.

A C Hartley (MMath)

Darren Coxon

Hayden Garrod (Kindergarten Head Teacher)

Husain Ghulam

James Anthony Thomas

Jill Monaco (MS Ed., SAS)

Jonathan Warner

Julian Edwards

Kevin Elliott (MEd, MBA)

Kevin Riley

Kim Marshall (former Boston principal)

Lynda Sharp

Matt Letham (MEd)

Michael Parent (Ed.D)

Paul Friend (MEd, BEd)

Paul Halford

Paul Michael (MA, MSc, FRSA)

Paul Williams (Head of Geography)

Peggy Burrows (MA (Hons) PhD Candidate; former Principal)

Philip Walters

Phyllis Campbell

Revalyn Faba Sack

Ryan Barbour (Deputy Headmaster)

Sharla Reynolds (M. Ed. Educational Consultant www.classnotchaos.com)

FINAL THOUGHTS

As the words of wisdom in this book attest, school leadership is challenging but incredibly rewarding. We need more wise leaders in our schools.

So, for those of you considering your first steps into leadership, for those of you considering promotion, and for those of your thinking of your first, second, third or final Headship:

> "EVEN IF YOU'RE ON THE RIGHT TRACK,
> YOU'LL GET RUN OVER IF YOU JUST SIT THERE."

Will Rogers

This book was never meant to be published. In fact, it originally started as my own private guide to leadership. I kept a notebook of the 'wise words' I heard in meetings, at conferences or in conversations.

As I rose up the leadership ranks, I started to share a few of the comments with colleagues: "*a wise person once said to me…*"

The positive response to those comments became the genesis for this book.

What I offer is a curated collection of thoughts and advice from a diverse group of school leaders. This book isn't a '*how to*' of school leadership. It's a '*how do*'. How do this sample of school leaders approach Headship, and what have they learnt along the way?

Their counsel has saved me years of wasted effort and frustration. I hope it can do the same for you.

May the wisdom herein make you a wise Head.

"A great companion to anyone's leadership journey. Dip in and dip out as the mood takes you for some quick snippets of wisdom."

"Short, snappy, impactful."

"Covers the full range of leadership. The highs, the lows, the stresses and the moments of joy.

"Provokes thought and offers practical advice; a rare combination" by the same author:

INTERNATIONAL SCHOOLS:
the teacher's handbook

Dr Denry Machin & Dr Stephen Whitehead

Examining and unpicking what it is to teach internationally – the highs, the lows, the perks and the pitfalls – this exciting new book is essential reading for anyone aspiring to, or living through, a career in international schooling.

Written in plain English, discover why international schools exist, the types of students who attend them, the parents who pay the fees, the pedagogical differences, the cultural challenges and the practicalities of teaching internationally.

You will learn how to find employment, or gain promotion, in an international school. Practical and easy-to-access, the book provides comprehensive insight into one of the biggest, and most exciting, career transitions many teachers ever make.